Eventually One Dreams the Real Thing

Marianne Boruch

Eventually One Dreams the Real Thing

COPPER CANYON PRESS

Port Townsend, Washington

Copyright 2016 by Marianne Boruch

All rights reserved

Printed in the United States of America

Cover art: Ben Marcin, *Morelia, Mexico* (2005)

Copper Canyon Press is in residence at Fort Worden State
Park in Port Townsend, Washington, under the auspices
of Centrum. Centrum is a gathering place for artists and
creative thinkers from around the world, students of all
ages and backgrounds, and audiences seeking extraordi-
nary cultural enrichment.

LIBRARY OF CONGRESS CATALOGING-IN-PUBLICATION DATA

Boruch, Marianne, 1950– author.
[Poems. Selections]
Eventually one dreams the real thing / Marianne Boruch.
  pages cm
ISBN 978-1-55659-491-5 (pb : alk. paper)
I. Title.
PS3552.O75645A6 2016
811'.54 — dc23

                                                    2015032450

9 8 7 6 5 4 3 2 FIRST PRINTING

Copper Canyon Press
Post Office Box 271
Port Townsend, Washington 98368
www.coppercanyonpress.org

again for David, first of all

Contents

Eventually One Dreams the Real Thing

Gift-Distant, Scratched

Maybe a pool filled with roses someone
uprooted before they bloomed fully.
And I stood before them the way an animal
accepts sun, the way an animal never
thinks hunger will stop.

It does stop. That's the best
I can say. You're given a life.
Each all every
small part can't be good, can't be
the worst of it.

For instance, I couldn't know why
such a terrible thing, roses wrenched out of earth like that.
They were floating.

But an animal—
to take in color like taste, flung petals drifting brilliant quick
savored, any human thought
somewhere distant, a scratched record,
the old turntable in the house
over and over, going bad.

Comes wonder in that sound.
Slip into a door
to lift the needle. Or full-faced as daylight,

stay in the yard.

I

Progress

These gargoyles can't get enough of the view
stuck to their cornice, ratcheting out
open-mouthed as some
desert hermit on his pillar, fifth century.

Such a vision, probably horrific. The gargoyles
take it straight to the river
over giant trees. A kingdom. If there is

a river. Or a kingdom. If I walk that direction—
how a lock knows its key, how the key's
little nicks and bites code fate: not *unlatch* but
continue, not *release* but *come through.*
Because it's ancient: there is
no progress, only a deepening. Or not even that.

I heard progress is a modern invention, post—
bubonic plague. Right up to the airplane, the double sink
and running water, earlier
the milking stool, and monogamy in some places.
But Dante leapt
at it, his *Purgatorio,* thanks to before, when—
wasn't it simple? Just heaven

or hell, friend. Sorry.
Thumbs up or down. Perfect weather or it's endless
awfulness.

How does it work, this new
Purgatory business, Dante didn't ask exactly
but dreamt first. Fabled searing
second chance lodged in the brain's ever-after

means to be left, reimagine, watch
whole bits burn off. Memory
needs sorrow. Even stone at its most
mend-and-loss molecular level moves, and the hard
secret parts of us know that: tooth, skull,
envy, the stubborn vertebrae, guilt worn down by
exhaustion, by despair you walk with,
and long enough. Like a month. Like years.

It's never simple. I learned what happened: gutters
replaced gargoyles. Those creatures sick of
siphoning rain off the roof with their long throats

stayed to scare evil out of the world, to be
merely beautiful and grotesque up there. Or they caution
back to us from the future, frozen
medievals, high-wire beings not of this earth
stretched, stunned to bone-limit, made possible again
by what they cannot bear to see. Now. Which is

lifetimes ago. I lose track of my transitions.

The Painting

Two brush-stroked boats, so-so weather, more detail
forward than aft, heavy
on shaded bits as
simple reflection, the mast dropping in water blurred.

Blur it more, gloom it up, says the teacher.
Use a rag and something stingy.
To look and look, is all.

Salt, fish air at dawn, turpentine. Or evening, that one.
To remember the past as
this painting remembers—beautiful, a little dull.
And maybe it was.

In fact, water can turn out demanding. Not staying put,
too much at odds in that glitter.
And people expect a quiet thing to hang on a wall
to forget their own noise.

That old guy bumming cigarettes for real
looked the part of another century, the ancient fisherman
contentedly mending nets in a time
with time to retie knots. So we
like to believe. And some would
sketch him right in, work him over like an afterthought,
historical. Better yet, to comment
ironic or just short of it. With him, without,
finally the worn reliable straightforward
sea, harbor, dream. Also this
for the record—three, not two boats. And those
warehouses weren't pink, didn't
watery-ache like the shadow they cast.

To be an artist, the best part—you, you're in
and then it's the same
but you're not the same. Smoke
from a factory on the other side, a small one
but billowing soot and ash anytime, a bad idea.
Or a good one, meaning
world. Which could threaten. Or end.
Go for a larger, darker resonance. The teacher
saying so says
never an extra boat either.

I heard things once, blurring out of sleep
or some other elsewhere to
none of us the same. The same what?
After. As in, *between* and *among* now
for a long time.

The Breathing

Think back with a shovel, bend,
do that.

Who's breathing through these tubes now?

So this is how you
plant trees in Scotland all afternoon.

We take instruction. The translucence
of it. Each plastic cylinder the exact shade of
a stem tall and suddenly wide, slipped

over sapling after sapling
sunk into earth, tied, staked against wind.
The mallet comes down.

January. A wee walk, we're told,
to get here. Fields this old,

the lives that lived. To ask anything

is to lose the question—
Hills plus sheep plus cold. Air like wet gauze
but sun, a bright accident.

Still: who's breathing through these tubes now.

I see plain enough, upright
nether-vents, their cool green
so many rows made

in the making. Barely trees at all
hidden, each incandescence.

It's the shovel, abrupt.
It's the fierce
stopped, to fierce again

the suck, the lift up
to go deep

a stunned thing.

It must draw them, the dead.
Both the violence and the ceasing must
remind them.

Because haven't they come
to lie here, their half-light just visible under
old stalks and grass. Dusk, with its

new dead and old dead…

And true, isn't it — that
we've pleasured them. True that our
hammering in breath

is another breath.

Not that I love you, the mouths they had
through oak, willow now, birch
will say —

a

They wore out the *a*
in the letterpress case only after
a few thousand hits under the inked rollers,
pulling the crank, turning
the giant wheel.

Must have been 1820. Thereabouts.
Wanderer, glory-run of letters: *thereabouts.*

Hunger took its due from
the belly of the *a*.
So? All kept reading it

as *a*—those who could read—and anyway,
a bite out of that apple proves
our kind mortal. Rare good paper
into page until most everything about the *a*
was shot. Practically prayer, humility,
a great foreboding not just
bare-bones frugal.

Simple *aaaa* from that *a*—
first letter loved, to hear it ache and fill
even at half-breath.

Look, it's standard. No one but
a divine being or two makes perfect copy.

Real case in point: my now-and-again body so
poorly echoed off my mother, my father
out of a broken skull simmering
in a bog, BC probably, long before AD

pretended anything in order. Earlier, our whole
dark hole of a planet copied
unto itself via earthquake, flood, star shard,
raging molten ball in the middle, some
big bang's idea
of a flawed, proper start.

For a while there, the tiny *a*
wounded. What it does.
Doing, to herald
every human sentence.

Aubade with Grass, Some Trees

Water on the ground and whatever will stay put
but I can't see that well. Or far.

What for, the deer out there. Not now. Not
with the rain. But two of them yesterday.

Even here, the sound of cars and their distance.

No song is complete without
some straying into the minor key but

what does such happiness mean. And who said
why first. And to whom, looking sideways

at what. Grass. Some trees. The furious shrill

of the legendary largest woodpecker
you almost never spot. I don't listen. I'm like

before I was. A stone. Or fish.

If a fish, how do I know the life in the pond
any different than the life in me. Mindlessness

is sweet. Oh this in-spite-of in the morning.
Because they forget. In captivity, round and round

the fishbowl radiant, willing.

In June

I can't help but
think about the dead. Everywhere
their flowers burn bright.

Roses lift the trellis, lie
about their thorns. Then the feather-like
lavender I can sweep

with my hand—that scent
wakes anyone. Oldest question,
oldest answer: so the dead

go where? A shrug,
a blank look. Or the stories
we've heard and heard,

nodded off hearing. There's a place.
There are angels, good
and bad, right? And we all—

Some of us fly. Fly!
I'd climb into the drawing
Leonardo made and be the figure

bent to gears
and levers and ropes pulling up wings
of tanned hide sewn

with raw silk. And fail. And never
get anywhere for years
and years. Talk to us,

the dead say, our
deep blues set the garden adrift,
our leafy fronds do the shade right.

Still one of the living, I walk there
twice a day, early morning,
evening. Because once

you made me lie down
in that dream, telling me
it's easy, it's all

in the small of the back, subtle,
most delicate angle. And you lift
like this, you said.

We're Not Insects

though we keep time, sort of.
And make our own
white noise. Ask the half-deaf who
lean closer, every word
bottom of a well, under rock and water
and here comes the bucket on a rope,
hitting the mossy sides
the whole way up, here where
cicadas begin in the body, all
its pools and deeps
and dusk. Insects that never
entered the garden by
invitation but their
triumph, their pulse and
their pulse—

Once Made of Feathers and an Ounce of Blood

From then on *Katrina*
fiercing up from the get-go
any girly girl named that.

Before too, whole phrases

incisor-sharp: fuck you, you fucking fuck!
all down the front. New Orleans,
black T-shirt sold on the street for mischief and joy
years back, pre-nightmare.

One has to respect
options, I said, three parts of speech
pressed into service.

Rage on fabric going, gone
redundant. End of the World, take that! A thing
to slip over your head.
Surely piles of them mouthing off on carts

to wild up later. Ever after. Day of days.

Torn wounded muck of it twisting out to sea,
great biblical sweeps: shipwrecked
porches, car parts in flight, dogs every

bent shape of
howl and horrific, dresser drawers
jet-streamed smithereens
beside warblers battered ancient into

once made of feathers and an ounce of blood.

You. If you ever wore
such a shirt, you'd hold it close,
a live explosive
under a milder, say, button-down.

And pause. *Oh yeah?* whipping
open, getting even.

Like some
Woden or Zeus seized. Grief

on steroids, if that were a god.

Notation Gregorian

after *Kyriale seu Ordinarium Missae,* author unknown

To note the inevitable is a most steady terrible job.
Diamonds pox the score, but the other puncta, little
square notes for the chant, many have tails
bedraggled kites can't get rid of either, the day officially
gloom now, treachery head-on in high wind.

Wily punctum: called *virga* and *often doubled*
thus the *bivirga, two quavers united by a slur.*
It's a quaver the throat knows, locked
in middle earth and ice. Beware.

But *the apostropha is never found alone,* e.g. —
in woods, where night falls
like a folktale. Not true! Famine is this
very soundtrack, the least-loved child left there
far from the river, a sacrifice, the yet-to-be bass clef
of any desperate mind. I'd grant
maybe a hungry second girl, both quavers
tap tapping it out.
If you think too hard down centuries about ways
we got here, you can't think at all.

Don't ask how an apostropha works finally.
Except I found a stray root in Greek: to turn, to turn away.
And a history of addressing
an imaginary person. In regard to
a repercussion is always to be made — agreed,
off whatever hard-hit note you
don't see coming, that faint echo down after each
keeps bruising. Minor —
never minor. And beauty
is blue black.

I guess one hears or
does not hear, an inborn thing like that dot to the right
of the square means pause because
I certainly understand hesitation, shame, embarrassment,
the world-without-end medieval underneath
brain, heart
my heart, stop, breathe. Ditto the plain English of
according to circumstances they may be sung
lightly crescendo or decrescendo. That's depending

on the angle of the stake in the heart put there by
god help us. And how huge
dark trees when
all is lost, those children dawned.

Song Again, in Spring

The bird's hunger, seeking shape: a worm shape, green
water bug shape passing out of
winter's clawed shape, its toothed shape where it
froze and stayed
freezing, the hawk up there, branch
or ledge, staring out and—

blink—down.

So be it
in the imperial age of the 21st century which seeks its shape
in the drone, the kind
put up to the killing, air-conditioned office turned bunker,
Nevada, home of the sand flea
whose life span is about two minutes the last
I checked though in truth,

I've never checked.

It's not a matter of just knowing.
Or that maybe the virtual bombardier is weeping at night
and feels bad about it.

Truth told
unto us: a worm shape is not
the worm. A worm, merely born to it like
an apple to its red eventually,
or the sea to its vast floating crosshatch of garbage,
plastic bags and cups from the big boats
and every who-gives-a-good-damn cute little
coastal spot, used-once forks
going brittle, snapping, drifting out to join their

cheap brethren, shining semi-continent of crap never
to decode/de-evolve/delete
for a thousand years if then, detritus of our time.

This *we,* this *our* and *us* thing —

A remote sensing device, garden path to a dark
darkest wood in the middle, etc. Confusion
as *part,* part coward, part crash
burning to quiet there.

Recalculate, recalculate, says the grown-up
robo-voice in the car, you've driven past your turn.

The turn was: *I want I want* alights on
oblivious, mouth-sized. Somewhere = sobbing.
It's spring! A thing with wings taking aim.

Long Ago into the Future

I get confused. So an acorn that
pretends itself for years into the giant oak
could nevertheless be windfall,
kaput. One night
does that. I've seen
clear evidence in the woods.

By the time the future hits, there will be a past
with our names all over it. Names
brought up from a distance
do have a solitary, universal ring to them: *here lies
whoever and ever.* Or whomever —
depending on how
the rest of the sentence goes, reversing fate,
subject to object not
seed anymore, not just-starting-out and maybe
that brave. The *such*

of such matters! The twilight way
it weeps or lucks somewhere to come
back there. Rooms,
various unveilings. To be so
infinitive about it — to spark, to hesitate,
all you want.

Divide

When elephants gather over a dead elephant
or crows above a crow ripped,
released by a hawk
or that cat online circling, lying down against
another cat still
so still—you're dreaming this, aren't you
bad dream? The room
shifts, the whole house stopped, one car
making its damaged
down-the-street a reverence.

When does grief become wonder?
To divide then, one part empty as the cocoon
a bagworm leaves on the stricken juniper
tight woven so beautiful
you'd never know its once-inside could
kill a thing this woody and pine-boughy and years
of its fragrance you walked by.
The other part—
all overflow get-rid-of-it,
grief unto wonder unto an offering
elephants bring huge in their delicate hovering,
their ridiculous tact, close
and closer, one cat
in vigil for another, sudden crows
quiet, a shatter no *cry cry*
winnows up.

Of course, explain. Of course they're like us.
Unless we're like them. And only when
words run and break apart and dissolve air
not even *air* anymore, breath

a rhythm, a backdrop—wait *in* wait, what's
left in us hopeless a long time for
the fallen one to move.

Beauty

at the Hunterian Museum, London

Not clear or this quite. But here's a glass case
hunger made. How anything digests.
Tiny circuit boards
eked out of

> ladybug
> bumblebee
> cricket   locust   leech.
> One grasshopper. One.

Or a young crocodile, or that sea cucumber's
rubber-band bits (no water, no wet, no blue,
no roaring). The intestinal worm's interior charms,
infinitesimal. A lizard
swallowed wildly too — a june bug took
that route, unlucky gnat after gnat after gnat.
Gastric runes of rat, of night heron, of reindeer.
The real inside skinny —
a single human fetus. On the spot
quiet. Middle shelf. For grandeur, for humility,
shock wired case-in-point.

Repeat sideways. To idle is to dream
by analogy. Something
like that. The one
could be many. Each dark night of little
gut machinery, same
turning thing into that other thing. Enter leaf, root,
flesh of world great and recognizable,
mangled, profoundly stranged, soaked, crushed
through gorgeous tubes, brilliant pockets to lift wings
minutes longer, a buzzing

made loud, claws gripping hard sand, hair to grow,
wounds to heal to
all right again. And rumblings so
raw, we who think we think this side of the glass
beauty — no,

danger, go first.
I mean I love enough my own
false prophets of supper and air, lost daily
down that channel once
newt small, trigger sharp as a silkworm's
click, about-to

ravenous —

In the Book of Myth

I believe first in the Scissors Man who disappeared
before the 8-track tape or the car it deafened.
That guy with his bell, thick
glittering stone jerry-built
to flip and lock so he could hover there, old ghost
over his grinding.

That bell: my mother
frantic at it, rummaging through drawers
for anything with an edge
not angry anymore. I'm dull,
says the knife among spoons, I want
it all back.

And what did we want out there
in the grass-middle of some
vast heroic, aping our fathers in an old war,
crawling breathless on our bellies.
Or Antarctica, a whole continent to be
discovered in the next five minutes before
we froze solid. Forget summer,
forget 85 degrees and house after house
the slow wet rhythm of sprinklers where childhood
can bore you to death. We'd slip
to a loose game of tag or statue-maker, the gradual
going dark, that renouncing of day,
the deep no-one-in-us-yet but a sound,
funny kink in wind
a ringing, fitful, the Scissors Man
up the street, getting bigger.

And exactly how: his half-bicycle, really
a cart fitted out with pedals, handlebars mummied up

in black electrical tape. A drawing
from a book, the half-horse, half-man guy traded up
for gears, for brakes, his one eye
that worked straining, stunned

into myth. Out of myth, I need to say.
Or if that's too easy, out of place then,
a real place, war and so
another war, a border, more borders and bribes
to a boat and a set of lousy
basement rooms at the end of it.
Just American children standing there—
that's the simple mist mist mist of it
to dim and flare *could*
or the *ever,* his one moment out of
how many lifetimes dragged behind as
right leg dropped and left leg rose,
the Scissors Man swaying,
breathing hard on his bike against
a bell's singing out.

Those few words he'd fling down like
coins of a city burned from the map, worn,
silver-heavy, losing the detail
of prince or queen, broken words of a grandparent
so familiar, speech
sharded to glass, back room of
rosary and missal, scent of cabbage, of sweet
sour wool. He'd stop.

And heave himself to the street. *You got?*
he shouted at our emptiness.
Your mothers got? waving back

to his grinding stone, his bandaged seat.

Prehistory

at the National Museum of
Scotland, Edinburgh

Which skull
to offer the gods first: pig or human,
or the sheep one, its bony black shield of a face
with horns stumping up, little
grand things. Or the twisting, hell-bent anthers
reclining, the rest of the reindeer lost.
Now do it. Patch in
eyes gone rigid in those heads
before the spear and then
the clubbing.

Shattered bowls in the glass case. And a sword
"deliberately broken." That word
deliberate, like the taste of blood surprises.

In return, the gods
do what?

Storms, good and bad. Life is short, or it's not.
There's luck and unluck. Reward, revenge.
Some gods breathe: that's oxygen.
One might throw a switch: that's spring.

Step out into time, it's hard
to know anything. Trains, their stalk of light
on a railway bridge,
the moon, the slow tide. Wheels burn and spark
if you could see
as gods do, in boredom, in anger, busy
with ancient simplicities: to let live or to smite—

Don't. Just look at him now.

Row 8, the sleeper at an angle against the window's
flash and flash off the bay, a rail's rhythm,
closed eyes, breath to breath

and grateful
for none of it on waking. Which of the gods spoke?
He won't remember. Threat held back —
still threat under glass, a few
broken things.

And beauty? Equals
the gods stare anyway.

He can't dream
the ticking weight of that either, afloat mindless
as fish are below.

The Ice Floe

Wind-weary stalks minus
corn. Full of August, bug-driven rags—
By winter somewhere, the oldies

pushed out on an ice floe, cold
yore of days. So it's said. So
it's said that it's said.

Put me there too! sings the immortal
nub in me, not much, watching
how all let go, one by every one.

The things we're told
when the undoing does—
parents, aunts/uncles, friends, beloved

spouses ever after, grandparents first
when you're little, each right
abruptly wrong and you're

eagled under, hiss-whispered
at the funeral: quit fooling around.
A day wherein *before* is

that's it, the *just before*
an horizon ready to welcome
this vessel flat as hope

taking wave after wave with
a person, this *once-was* on top
not waving, I assure you.

A Bat in the House

swoops high, webbed little arms for
not quite a figure eight, prefers
a big room, out open windows into dark's
usual happiness,
insects for supper, where roost—

So much light in here, sealed shut awful,

the bat's radar
screwed up by fear and its
haywire. *A drunken spree:* what they said—
old movies, the gray
of black and white, actors thin,
elegant, looking out

to a garden without color,
drawing delicately on cigarettes to take apart
the incident, to underscore,
to amuse—the falling down, the blurting out.
Martinis in hand, just a splash, an olive.

Wayward whirl of

smoke on set—the director too,
the cameramen, even
the best boy-not-a-boy. What passed for
having a thought, the deep drag
to take warmth into the lungs, the glance up

to consider release, the meaning in

a glass broken, whether roses, how to figure
who's standing where
to be shocked at what. Not the bat,
real. Or the blind

infinity he comes from, my human

sick at heart—don't I know him by heart?—
suspended, shrunk to the net as
the long pole comes down,

expatriate, sharp-toothed dazed messenger.

Doing that Thing to the Field

Fog lies down on a field though it's

not the field sleeping. Maggot and leafworm
fury all night. Early light

is a dust-up of light. And the fog

isn't cloud, isn't
heaven come to earth no matter

what it looks like.

Last, before bed, news on every channel
of news: the air show,

one clip, the crash

no sound at all. In human hands, the camera
skews it, the pilot old too.

And from a picture book of anything that flies,

like a child might draw a plane,
tiny black business behind each reporter's

big talk-talk—across, flaming down

a blunt right angle those
stations kept, keep playing

into dream's little smoke.

Then the grandstand part,
the expensive box seats.

The fog, doing that thing to the field.

How could I know it was
out here. Already in afterlife when I thought

of coming out here.

Mudfest

Some kid in the class,
a boy usually, Do we have to, Sister?
And the nun once: no. She turned and slowly *no, you don't*
have to do anything
but die.

A room's hush
is a kind of levitation. So the end of a rope frays. So mortality
presses its big thumb into clay early, 6th grade,
St. Eugene's School, midcentury.
It's a mudfest, ever after. Free, yay! is what some heard
howbeit the gasp
primal, a descending, an unthinkable click.

Forget what she'd no doubt been
programmed to say, as postscript, as speaking-of: but we live forever,
don't we, children? in God's sweet light?
She didn't. Too old, too mean, too tired, too smart, maybe shocked
at her own relish, her bite coming hard.
I'm just saying there are
charms on the bracelet from hell.

An ordinary question, the boy's whatever it was, and did we *have* to?
He was stunned. I could tell.
And he must have walked home in the falling leaves distracted,
disturbed, pushed off for a time
from the anthill.

As for the other ants, we had our work.
It gleamed like truth is said to, in the dark before us —
grains of edible filth or just
sand and splintered glass. To carry.
Carry it down.

The Mermaids

The spell is a mouth's
perilous-o as they dark circle the boats in
their most resplendent pliable armor.

The concept *fish* aligning with *girl*
or love with death
to bring down men at sea, temptation

confused into *offering,*
the mismatch of like plus unlike
really likes, straight to rock-bottom.

No equation has ever been this badass.
It's the men who will enter the spell
so far into exhaustion as weather, as waves,

the tide pulling toward *if,* letting go *then*
over the whale road in the company of
the dolphin, the only other animal, I'm told,

who can do it solely for pleasure. It.
You know what I mean. The lower half
aglitter, the top half brainy as beautiful

is sometimes, murderous lovelies, their plotting
and resolve and why not
get these guys good, the lechers.

To see at all in the whirling, to hear
what anyone might
in wind roar and faint whistle—

Don't worry about girls shrewd
as whimsy, legend-tough
to the core. Don't. But it's

their spell too, isn't it? Locked there.
Aligned with singing, dazzle
razor-blackened green. Not that they

miss what *human* is like or know any end
to waters half born to, from where
they look up.

Men in boats, so sick of the journey.
Men gone stupid with blue,
with vast, with gazing over and away

the whole time until same to same-old to
now they're mean. After that, small.
Out there, the expanse. In here,

the expanse. The men look down. Aching
misalignment — gorgeous
lure that hides its hook steely sweet

to *oh my god,* little fool's breath
triumphant, all the way under and *am I
not deserving?*

Triptych in Grief and Life-Glad

I

I get sick of birds the way I get sick of jokes, their punch lines ready to spring.

And that expectant luminous look on the face you have to mimic back.

The way I get sick of the killdeer fighting out there on this vast lawn where I've

landed like a Martian, startled how different my language is, so keep to myself,

never attempting talk even with the sad stripped bird in the fury, those two

in their battle. It's the big fancy one who wins. Thicker stripes, ferocious

the way his beak comes down on head, on feathers. Early morning, late afternoon,

ground zero for their get-on-with-it: berries, insects with other ideas,

twigs, fluff for the nest somewhere, mine all mine. Somewhere was never Mars.

So I came to Earth and hear birds deafen me with their cacophony though

I'm fond of the word *ca-coph-o-ny,* its pauses that knife little hot air balloons.

Exactly confusion, and the shrill nerve required of any utterance

from the underworld. They're at it again. The sad one forgets he will lose

and I root for the sad one because we both forget.

2

Because we both forget, the girl I was and now this grown-older whatever,

I happen on a thought. The thought takes a train north. Or it wants

back to its box, thank you. The little chip for a soundtrack embedded

up near the corner is faulty, keeps shorting out the Brahms when it rains.

Okay. I'm not Martian. And I relish jokes. I *loathe* Brahms, someone told me

the other day unprompted. A lot starts that way: inexplicable.

Like the girl I was fifty years ago, oblivious in the plum tree backyard that

flowered in May like some mad-scientist invention spitting

popcorn or tickets for the time machine. My mother loved beauty as brief

before her one marble, then another, then all of them lost. As for Brahms,

I pointlessly pointed out he played cheap honky-tonk in a brothel in Hamburg

when young. To be young! As if that could lift disdain's thousand pounds — see,

he could do anything. Later I thought: maybe a tavern, not a brothel. Maybe

I misspoke. Later I'm corrected back, where I started. But so much isn't

or either. The sea air, the sting, since Hamburg is a harbor.

3

Hamburg *is* a harbor. A city of bridges, someone happily warned me,

more than Venice, she bragged. *More than* is one of those nifty devices to measure.

Like lunatics weigh the body before and after for what's gone. The soul,

three-fourths of an ounce! In school I pictured that almost-an-ounce a tooth suspended,

a stain, under my ribs. Nuns told us. You had to brush it. And midway through his

monsters and his languishing, what if Keats did say soul-making the why

life on the planet, first place, last place. What if those words—*planet, soul, life*—stopped,

right here. Then you are in fact from Mars disbelieving, point zero amazed the distant

blue at fault, music's rise and drop, the deadly reverence over dumb things, quarrels

to be at all. I can read. And put it in real time yesterday. Russia, in Stalin's freeze.

One detail: the hard-boiled egg Mandelstam eats before they take him away. Meant for

another, another poet, that egg he roamed streets to find, carried back, an offering

delivered out of its roiling. Gracious. On the table. But his wife, his friends, insist.

II

Water at Night

Not that I understand things.
Angels don't walk toward the ship, old engraving
where moon throws
a river of light, how angels would walk the ocean
if they wanted to walk.
They don't. They hover. A lot of space
between them and what
shines like waves. Which can't
be a choice, for angels or
the engraver who was in fact
Gustave Doré after sleeping off
the ancient mariner Coleridge left behind under
guilt and regret and an albatross' weight.
Which isn't much, but they are
big animals, four feet across counting
the wind involved
and rain. Doré waking to a room not
really of wings. I guess
a stirring, something in the black expanse
he hoped to razor into
the copper plate — no, a graver,
not a razor at all.
Beauty does terrify, a bare nothing
but stop. As in angels. Abrupt.
Still, to cut them their flight on metal
takes a while. His hands stiff,
Doré under a deadline no doubt like the small
endlessly later rest of us
do what we do and do until
it's not what we do.
Nevertheless, angels. Why did they
keep coming, one by one radiant

dark of a mind paused to
this most desolate given: water at night.
That it floods a future not
even in the picture.

Dickinson in the Desert

Repeat. No trees. Repeat.

How it spreads. Vast bronze, burnt orange to ocher
to unsettling. Clouds scatter-deepen
thought or no thought dazzled to a cactus
red-flowering all over the place low,
not quite a heart into shards.

She might love this. Then she does, she's doing

and I say: why? And Dickinson: why wouldn't
I be here? My needle and thread, my
words to fit pages I cut
and make little books no bigger than my hand
to hide in this spot of future weirdly
uneventful, just like before,
in Amherst. I'm crazy curious, remember?

Her hand, any hand wired up
to the sparking furious brain cannot sleep.
I've read that much. It's the ache of trees I miss.

You're here in the desert not even a week,
she says to me, you've seen
the hot hours, then night's lovely-cool
under a blanket. She's making conversation,
upbeat as the 19th century gets these days.
She shrugs. Of course.

Wait. Dickinson—shrugging!

By now it's dark, vast
down to *vague,* word of no color.
She's staring—

The desert takes a turn: forget what I was,
forget that.

Dickinson in Snow

No sound from the start or
words just give way. Must be
rage in it. Perhaps I made that up,
her windows surely dark-deep in its crepe
months on end

and probably her never the proper shoes
like men got.

In summer, her stab at wit, part unkind,
part prophecy. That story, an old woman confused
trying to get home, stopping to ask
bewildered, and Dickinson—
down there, turn left, that's right—matter of facting her
straight to the graveyard.

My grandfather called such a place
a marble orchard each time we passed its
calmest eye and stones
spiring up near fields. So many chiseled names
weathered to unreadable. And closing in,
the busy self-absorbed corn.

But snow is snow. Dickinson in it
no matter what season. Blank as
years from now, any page
before any words. And the past
coming down in silver flakes, like after some
terrible fire, all that ash.

A low whistle at night. Might as well
be snowing. Sleep on that train,

strangers only dreaming awake, awake —
their triumphs sufficient or never,
not in this life.

Dickinson in the Woods

So it is under the world. She and I pass the time.

Done, Dickinson says. I wrote like a multiplication table
equals what?

What is what we still open, I tell her.

Little swarms! Those poems came at me.
I had no headgear, no fancy moonsuit between
me and their mesh. Some claim I put
too many hives in the shade, that I got it wrong—
bees love sun.

Here, I say, some peppermints to shatter
the dark mouth cold. And they sting.

My body isn't anymore. But thank you.

Her thank you—
was that so surprising? Or how I cherish it.

Woods get quiet. Midafternoon won't draw down
like dusk, isn't fragile or birds. Barely, her

you hear that?

Dickinson and the Future

Sure, but she's — what was the word once? —
indisposed. As in: come back later.
She's sewing a wren together
which is hard. It keeps trying to fly. She's intent
as that time she turned the dove inside out
to fix it. And found a snake there.

I definitely need glasses
to do this one, Dickinson says, though already
she admires how feathers
hook together against rain, plus the little wren beak
she might speak to
and from, were she that sort of poet.

Those jottings: inscriptions on a tomb.
Again, this minute! Her rigging, her loops.

Define *unknowable* for me, she thinks to
ask the bird anyway, define *door,* define *key.*
Not a chance, given the wren is
almost, and if things do work out
it's mostly forget after.

To be mesmerized, pause and future pause
which takes to itself each
darkening eye —

The dove at a loss now
is fine, still singing dread, how sorry,
sorry sorry everything
not the least of it.

Dickinson's Twenty-First Century

Because she never could. Can't
resist urgency, a phrase, a fable that's true...

For instance: two ghostly lovers who
do not forget, two chairs with
their imprint each morning, a grand
salon in the desert, oldest house around here,
every night shattered glasses, knives
thrown to the floor no
motion detector picks up. The docent says so.

It's D (if I may) dimly, and close: *I never stop thinking.*

That's the famous human what
to see in this town, I tell her, brochure in hand: the 1850s,
the poor two of them, their names even —

Astonished, her *mo-tion-de-tec-tor?* is her
pulling thick taffy to my
saying it. But no one does that anymore,
whatever steamy-sweet kitchen I know.

Still it comes to her, the 21st century. She's mouthing it,
and best, for them: *Motion detector!* — beloved
Armando, oh Inez. A warning to the cohort, very slow

keep yourself hidden.

The Class of 1940

Winds blew through my mother, maybe all of them
off sleeping fields, snow then clear,
small town to big town. Only a short trip.
Not really. *Took over an hour.* Her buddy Ruth,
twins Sally and Bill, 30 miles each way
in the borrowed Ford, the boys to graduate
to no clue, my mother — *I'm telling you,
fun!* — crammed next to

Bob Edie, next to Harold, sweet on
the both of them, one
our could've-been-father
my brother pointed out across a parking lot
while we made up house, yard,
a life with the other, our almost-father too,
backass genetics as if
the chief circuits of our world could change and we'd
be spit out same and same. Her Harold shy,
a serious sort, though the story, Michener's Dry Goods
she part-timed after school, his
picking up a huge brassiere, all lace and full cups, draping it
at his widow's peak, and down: *Look Martha, earmuffs!*
So out of character, my mother said.
Love that, she meant.

Big bands in the larger town, and dancing.
Plus the standard wise-guy stuff — the teasing, the jokes,
the drive back that time, faint press of coat sleeve,
of hand out of glove, plain young nearness to relish,
their two-in-the-morning finally separate beds, separate stops,
slipping off in the dark, each
porch light, its 40-watt dim. *The gang,* she so fondly.

Her mother's hot cocoa, whatever
hour the end of it.

From here: boys
with a war waiting. And after, what facts if
at all from them. Normandy. Burma, those men
down to 90 pounds heaving stone at gunpoint.
Once, rare blurting out at a funeral,
the camps: *so goddamn terrible,*
just charred human firewood is
what we saw.

Is that how it works? A shared run of grief
is a veil and a mute. First a no-going-back big X where
time crosses place to blast
and slow burn and blood up and scare shitless.
Equals empty. As in
how to say about that, *how to say,* whole rest of a century.

But why tell us anything? So what if those left
still self-medicate with rage or spite, some with happiness
really sorrow no one can reverse, in disguise.
They've shot themselves with holes or gotten so old.
Some forget. That was my mother, her habit
of innocence gone rigid, not loss but rounding down
and out before any history in there
caught. Just — *we had*

a big time, locking herself in a room with it
gifted, blown back to
permeable, thoroughly ghosted by then.

Aubade with Bird

Late fall, one of them doing
a half-assed job of his singing into early,
this not-light yet. He's mostly pathetic.

Or too young to know better, a teen bird
testing limits, pretending
to claim territory. Or *love me, love me,*
come feathered thing. Definitely his
jumping the gun on that. And of
the real cold to come, its ice
and froth, or the hawk's bellyache written in blood,
he's got no blessed clue.

Practice, practice night
all night turning to any day now.
You can see it lift. Not a curtain but that bird
runs through his lines whatever,
the first Hamlet until
Shakespeare gets to the theater, tells him
straight out furious, the world's weight
is the wording—
                Dark. Little dark
just before.

The Young Husband

All vision is
peripheral. Under an eave
the young husband on

his cell to his wife, talking, smoking,
not talking, no longer waiting
to tell the strange part,

the funny part, not
in that order, he says at the door.
So like you

once telling me: peripheral. Loss of
detail and color sideways
except for what shifts to—

How long that takes, sudden.
True and true, not
only true, my old enough

to be moved by
anything, the mainly
all-of-this-not-me. Rain,

a little. The cool spring night.
Three cigarettes (down to
one a day really),

this new young husband
is saying, because
they've been texting

because it's good to talk finally.
Just and like and so
a face, lit

out of the weather —
Weren't we? The body
loves that.

Book and Screen

It's mostly someone
long dead who gets curious
all over again, who once told
a book, the book
picked clean to glow
on a website now, an address
with double slashes in it.

Suddenly I love
one detail: the way they harnessed
horses or hammered
copper, what seed—cardamom, rye—
kept its small heart aloft
for a millennium.

Voices in that
dark ago when I open
to room light, lamp
or window on book—old friend—
or the new computer screen.

It's not technology, either way.
It's something
in the brain first, an inkling. *Not yet
yours to know.* Behind that

little hallways in
sleep. The walking,
the every door.

RE:

I said okay okay and then it was
altogether right to say
all right, I said. Though on the other hand,
I said. Just that you understand how
this is, I said at least twice.

And considering, taking fully into account the matter of
could be, soon a might
have been, it's at least partly wise to upend, see
what second thoughts, last minute to relish!

Sound of heating duct, printer not printing, my own
temporal artery in the nothing they said.

Right. Or it was that other
else I blurted at the table. Something like: I imagine
it's possible though we may need

more time, what with and as it happens, whoever
and beyond aren't there other means to
other ways to pledge ourselves one starry planet
in the cloud bank?

Well, sure, I guess I said then

over the quietest perfect falling
into place or pieces.

Big Little

Brain leans toward the heart: *I can't hear you!*
It's not a given. Every day
is different as clouds. One's a rabbit
in half-leap
over some interesting clover.
A second cloud's small
as a bee glommed to that sweetening before its
radar's knocked off by a teenager's
cell phone over at Walmart. *O hive,*
where art thou? Here, says the brain, right here.

So the brain is
a serious racket, buzzed as rain in a drought
or rain in the middle of rain or three
whole Tuesdays of rain.
The heart too
is complex. Its emphatic narrows to fuse up
the worst possible
chick movie. Or some action film, its thud thud
in the hero weighed down dumb
to really dumb by armor, his faux glory so long ago
it was yesterday. Maybe he can
learn something from grief.

Heart and brain: which one of them
wants more? All is realm, a theory of realm
vs. realm. But it's fun, thinks
a thought, give me a try!

The brain, what a liar. Not desire, all's
free fall to the most common denominator, only
keep beating the brain wires down to

the obsessive, cheerless heart.
I'll figure you out, I promise, the brain keeps
stage-whispering south toward

that thicket. *Promise.* Such a big
little word, the heart
lost and clutch and release.

The Pulse of the Nation

Could be a plot. Or just backdrop—
the soap operas on TV, all timed

to the pace of ironing, most wakeful hours
in robot-land, tranquilizer slow unto

sure and I told you, didn't I? Now sleep.
There went my childhood, my mother

complaining the McCarthy hearings
knocked out her programs. *The Secret Storm,*

as if a garden glade howbeit duplicitous,
and her favorite, *The Guiding Light*

not quite a glorious shaft off a holy card's
stained glass in the big clunky set

my father got discount. I'd ask her—
what was it like? The country

paranoid-berserk, Joe's eyebrows up
insidious at every alleged

Commie-crazy in monotone pleading
the fifth. Her hands flew: maybe eight weeks?

Not fair! Her soaps off the air as he reigned
and raged. Make no mistake. My mother

had her finger on the pulse of the nation.
Which is music really. I see those women

ironing—thousands back there hypnotized,
worn down by the rhythm, curious

solace and drug to keep a world kept.
I claim no vision. But old bowling shows too,

a lulling brainwashed over-voice
evenly feigning high drama

to hold back: *Now he picks up the ball, now
he aims, he steps forward, now*

it's rolling— Strike! No, a spare! Then all
went dead as the long-toothed grille for the pins

came down distant like they still
teach you to draw perspective, to sweep

all troubling complication. Some
dodgy art class, also on TV.

Little Handheld, Little Movie in a Phone

This boy this boy this boy walks
into woods because
a dog goes deep — you barely make out
her dappled light.

This wee boy, the Scots would say, so?
Just rushing where the beloved went.

A father's words fainter, a mother back there who
sees, holds the little handheld, patiently

world! meet this marvel of a boy
darker, dark wavering beyond
earshot still
corner-of-an-eye distant
sun in trees mostly shade, the dog rolling around
as a dog will

for joy, a blur, what the hell. A boy
between, leaf in layers
a breathing, his alone own
breath away from, ahead, oh the gods as
double whammy, the one called
Further, the one called *What a Life to Be Had.*

Delicious. Dangerous
glorious ever after: keep going! ecstatic
in that dim and just so great —

Or a singing. Aren't they always singing?
Their names too: *Stop, Turn Back,*
Oh Thick of It Give Way, three

quieter gods.

Stray, Repeating, Human

Bear down: a pencil's more miles
than dream-rapid sprung, hardcore trek of its
waking life on paper. I do know
you sharpen to go forward,
turn a crank, little razors inside. Erase, erase.
Every mindless touch counts—
                                    Go birth yourself
crazy. To a stub.
Fifty thousand words, give or take, per pencil.
I'm pelted every day
by factoids. Word unto word unto word.
Beloved kenning of the ancients,
their double slap of "twilight-spoiler" equals
dragon when sea-hardy sorts hit the "swan-road"
at a pretty fast clip. That's *Beowulf* for you, spooky
with enthusiasms.
                        There are limits.
Tell the pencil again—
fifty thou, that's it. Suffer the world
to eke through. Bravo to the stray repeating human,
centuries to stuff graphite inside
a skinny wooden shaft: poems, stories, grocery list.
Wow. To make anything at all, be it
moonlight or a shrug.
                            Take up your weapon.
As in, the pen—
surely the pencil—is a sword is a sword is a sword.
No, mightier! Stock slogan, bulletin board,
bleak waters of 8th grade, cheesy ya-ya claim
could, it could
raise a ship caught rock-wise, inland
ice-age sea just as

a storm blew over the sword business, the room, pen
a corny feather pen dipped in ink,
landlocked Midwest.
                               Afternoon, a pencil
stepped up
in spite of me *fathom* *wet dark* little razors
glittering millennium on
millennium — *astonish*
quick to slow jolt
and fall. I mean years.

When I Think about the First Pope to Quit

that job, 1294, five months in
since summer, almost Christmas, Celestine the Fifth
and how before: *We need*
an honest man and you're it, Pietro da Morrone, the cardinals
in their red-lavish showing up at his cave, he
having visions enough, eating grass in between,
no, shaking his head *no*—a lot of good
that does.

Abducted to elegance, proper meals, a table, real
linen under the suddenly rich look of him, he
wasn't anymore. Or hardened further, a nub quite
outside himself—though there is no self—shiny as a star
he'd turn away from every time, big windows
or no windows.

And why do I go quiet and thrill to this decoder ring
in the cereal box, nuns telling us
squat everything else back to zero, the old days,
little desks, sit up straight.

And why are the long days so short?

The brain is a superpower of play and replay. Certain moments.
That poor man in his ecstatic loneliness
digesting his impossible porridge of weeds and sticks
looks up again to who is that
down the rocky crevice, how they tripped and cried out like
babies or the black bird,
held on to each other trying for regal and upright,
a colorful flash, a feast
out of hell to tempt him. Was it

just the flattery? Their bloated want
narrowing to his
least, nothing left to say.

Yes goes so far. Then it stops like time
before clocks got invented by someone who heard
madness, the small deliberate what
isn't, what is
no. Last. Larger for it.

Song in Winter

January. But it's spring
for an hour—rain,
not snow. Then sun, not cold
or too cold. No shock when the door
opens. No sucked-up breath, no
stalactites or stalagmites in there, no cavern
of moist ruins, rock slides or cave-ins where ribs
keep guard, where lungs catch or can't quite
and go atonal as you slept and where
I worried. *Beautiful* winter, repeat that
in this dream of winter, wounded

dazzle and freeze. Only—
to open a door, to breathe right so wrong out of sync.
Asthmatics! Rise up! Put down your inhalers!
This *yes*
without logic, as if there were
reason. Doom is
or it isn't. I didn't have to say.

Piece of Old Cornice among Trees and Random Trash

Just lying in woods, once
fired to thick terracotta now partial, part shattered
as a sentence dropped midsentence because

everyone else left the room. Or it's a verb
back to its infinitive lonely,
theoretical: to believe, to give up,
oh, to lie down.

How story is made: I saw the bigger part
of whatever it came from,
neighbor to the old blistered sink, and maybe it really
was a mantel upon which certain
aspirations leaned like people with meaningful envy
and late afternoons to kill with
a nice drink before dinner.

The standard oak leaves carved into it when
clay at first, innumerable various fruits not quite
recognizable. Even so, an honest shard of still life
though the old Dutch painters would have warmed up
such a vision with a half glass
of wine — safer than water — and added mystery
by way of a few torn feathers. Not the piece I found
with its little pockmarked shield still
emboldened between what
might be grapes.

Which is to say this fragment accepts rain in the dump
as an offering, years of rain behind that, no less.
There's wealth. One suggestion can
equal elegance. There's why
and why again I get

trapped working from a detail, blowing it up intact
where fine and regal lived
in an actual house, the well-appointed kind with
zero zero zero
nod to me and most as in
the likes of
multiplied, inevitable, underfoot. They say
so it goes. And it does.
But what if

an argument broke out. Or it's about to break
in real time or by telepathy
you can see in all the faces. Small condescensions
razored off in such a house at that mantel
as fallen snow-blinding chaff
on the one standing in

for the ravaged, so secret to begin with—
Nothing. The perennial always-thus nothing for it
but to will

the hammer down on the perfectly made thing.

Hospital

It seems so—

I don't know. As if the end of the world
never happened in here. No smoke, no
dizzy flaring except those candles
you can light in the chapel for a quarter.
They last maybe an hour
before burning out.
                    And in this room where

we wait, I see them pass, the surgical folk—
nurses, doctors, the guy who hangs up
the blood drop—ready for lunch,
their scrubs still starched into wrinkles,
a cheerful green or pale blue,
and the end of a joke, something about a man
who thought he could—
                    Down the hall and

laughter, to spill like that.

Dr. Arthur Conan Doyle Back from the Dead, Talking
   Endlessly on a Tiny TV

He says in the newsreel
a hundred little dodges
to make his Sherlock Holmes think straight,
meaning crooked, meaning sense and surprise do mix.
A museum thing. Surgeons' Hall, Edinburgh —
bones in bottles, flesh ravaged by disease or musket balls
or plain bad DNA, O chloroform save us,
carbolic soap and Lister Lister Lister, now
Conan Doyle, homeboy
of this old and gorgeous city.

It's just that, holy jealous! His detective
gets mail. One young woman would drop her darling
village boy to marry him. Holmes,
that is. The doctor should be saying: yes, my stilted prose,
yes, rare luck of the draw, a great character
came to me. Dogged effort pays off.
Everything's a mystery until
a narrative kicks in.

You know what? It's still a mystery.
Such a small screen. The film scarred, badly lit, on repeat.
I sit in a chair, watch
the big man welcome the camera as I imagine
he rose to the wide-eyed patient who's
quite forgotten why she came or what is wrong.
That sweet blank stare of the lens
is hers. Now it's mine.
But he hasn't practiced for years, outdoors in the footage,
blurry shade, the late '20s, his
my stories, my novels and what to do, and how

do it and not doctor all day, and so on
and so forth

to 1929. Where my mother turns eight
in the mind's eye behind him,
or the stock market—hear that crash?
Disaster comes. And it goes. Probably
a flower bed
the real backdrop, and shade means
an oak or wych elm, a house,
wicker table for tea, this loop this loop this loop…

So much is plain exhausting
and exacting and every stupid reason loves its reason,
those hundred little dodges that
get us in the end.

Sir Arthur, my name is
Merely and it's Dust Mote, it's Future and Gray Dissolve
where time put me in this chair
to watch you by accident because
so what. Or who knows. And no telling.

Old Words

My word! — as if
stunned. That and
grip for suitcase, both in the fossil record.
Maybe even *suitcase* now.

I almost get it, my
grandmother's *why, don't that beat bobtail?*
for honest-to-god wonder.
The *why* in there — to consider, not
to question. How dear is that
in the 21st century?

Also. I'm fond of
of an afternoon, how it opens to
filling station across the street where
a real house,
it used to be that
rather lovely one, the ritual of retelling
the bad news, its going down,
the silence behind *what's gone is gone.*
A *stout* fence. Daylilies.

No one cares really.
No, I don't mind that.

If in a store once or
many times, her small stooped body,
whatever old woman out of habit —

Some movies
are terrible, the cornball parts
the worst.

Private Garden, Open to the Public

Down, left of the fountain facing where they lived,

In memory of the children
of this house

—late 1800s, whatever years. Nevertheless
the triumphant life-sized Christalan atop a giant stone
in his short dress right out of the Middle Ages

looking forward to the Renaissance, his arm
raised of course, ending in a thumb pretty much gone,
an index finger missing, the other three
crooked, at rest.

That forefinger, maimed by mistake
or banished. Once straight up
swearing allegiance to a bleak hopeful heaven

if I can fortune-tell the past as the future might be
whose rain is now, on my bike
and I'm soaked

as memory gets, all its bits whirling about
in an old brain. You could
so-what grief
and dumb down. One could
so do that—

Never going to look better than we look right now!

a friend in an e-mail, something she read
to wry up, to blurt into the saddest e—outer space
a voice I superimposed, in my head

I could just hear her. The fountain on—Spring!—
and making an effort.

It Moves

at the American Academy in Rome

Late evening. Galileo showing off
his telescope again, a ring of murmuring
at our window. The very spot
and year, 1611 —
So goes the addiction to marvels, as in
maybe now, if only…

Chilly for Rome, in spring, these nights to see far away
through a lens and a tube.

It ended badly, that Earth-around-the-sun thing.
The Inquisitor, heresy, the recanting, etc.,
except that parting whisper at the door *but it moves* is how
his fame works.

It moves. You Aren't The Only One In The World—
a mother's muted-loud
word by word like breath held
is released or
teeth wait to come down.
And Earth not by a long shot the fearless
frozen-in-place center of it all.

Well done, Galileo.
Good job, planet reliably doing rounds
day into night, eternal tit for tat,
a winter summer spring fall that will not stop.

Light years aren't really. But imagine
a dead radiance speeding back
when you're old suddenly: Sorry, you've

used them all up, Starship. It's large like that.
So what if we're not the bull's-eye of every wonder—

His year, his day, I dream a Galileo
stunned by many things but *here's my proof*
hung to their silence, the worst.

Just this: I'm in the long process of
thinking a telescope back
to a circle of glass slowly ground into foresight
and hindsight, Galileo
months in a shed in Trastevere until, look up!

But it moves —

Little fruit trees and lettuce and *broccoletti,*
a bit of wind all night. A murmur still a murmur
then no sound at all. Out there
a garden now.

Before and Every After

Eventually one dreams the real thing.

The cave as it was, what we paid to straddle
a skinny box-turned-seat down the middle, narrow boat
made special for the state park, the wet, the tricky

passing into rock and underground river.

A single row of strangers faced front, each of us
behind another close
as dominoes to fall or we were angels lined up
politely, preflight, like that was
a coffin we rode, the go-to, take-out end of it,

a shipping container for a giant.

Now every after—
Not to embellish, but I count the Ice Age in this story
since its grinding *made* that cave.

I count us too, as mourners.

A smart, full-of-fun-facts park ranger poled us
past summer. A cool which meant dark, meaning
I pictured the giant in life before
he lay down in that boat

under the blood in us, under our breathing.

Upright, his long bones
and knobby joints. He slouched in a doorway
smoking cigarettes, talking What-Would-Bertrand-Russell-Do

kindly and funny to the dumb
all of us who adored him, not dream and then dream.

Repeatedly, that thing about us adoring him.

The ranger pointed out the obvious
spare mob scene of caves: the endless drip to make
a stalactite, tiny crawfish and frogs transparent, hearts
by flashlight, visibly beating away.

We got quiet drifting deeper.
What does it mean, again and again
with your eyes shut?

I remember us from before too,
from museums. I love us there still, the same
us, the way the ancient Egyptians kept their dead
safe crossing over, smallish
intricate models — who they were and even

their sorrow to scale — those rowing tireless

to the other side. A boat the length of my forearm,
faces to freeze like that
forward, released to the blankest wonder though
I think we came back. Of course he did not

and could not, the giant

I made up for the passage. But all night
the whole dream
grateful I was to others
patient, more steely practical with
things sacred, who took the real one across

hours before we got there.

III

Singular

Most true that bird, most singular
though many birds, oddly a flood of them
come yard, come late, come now. Maybe a downy, his scared
little run-down riff. Some lonely one of them. Winter descending
is also a singular dark.

Most true, your voice. I can spot it even dimly, as in: the phone
in someone else's hand across the room. A singular
talent of ear. Plus, after thirty-some years: I know you best, don't I?

Singular: the first scribbling, printing off, holding the page, scratching out.
Retype, rehum the printer. Singular: the many glimpses so
slightly shifted to compel, to hypnotize the you in you —
you had no idea... Such a private act. Write, reconfuse, resettle
outside to inside, unquiet pinned to paper
is singular, if not delusional.

Most true and singular and nearly my same lunch every
singular day. Pleasure can be
small. How the tasty
full-of-itself on a plate vanishes: down the hatch, they say,
all changing en route to
an inglorious fate. That wickedly ruined end-of-things starts
toasted and modest, so bread and cheese. Close,
emblematic, a very low form of ironic.

I still do that, iron. I call it my i-ron, my i-ron-ing board. As in
have to do a little i-ron-ing now. Doing some
irony here. Pressing lightly, this heavy
hot thing in hand just a second, to get things straight. That's physical,
"tongue in cheek" though no one's tongue
lives there long. I like best the Brits saying *cheeky. Well, that*

was rather cheeky of you. In fact, I love how the Brits
across the blue-black sea-monster sea
say at all, like my friend, how
his old addled mother had been *living with the fairies for*
some time now, like how I kept hearing don't worry, we'll get that *sorted,*
we'll *look after* whatever-it-is: you, me, someone, many
someones not even in the family though I'll
never get that *royal* thing, *the royals.* Wholesale blank-check
reverence as a national hobby just isn't
the right happily ever after — *not bloody likely* — where we think so hard

singular. Here. Look up.
One airsick feather coming at you.
Fewer birds.

Never Body

is night's body, is
out of body. I knew that early.

Find your spot,
I was told many times. She meant
getting into bed, turning this way, that,
settling in like the first snow before
any dreaming up snow.

Remember? Weigh nothing.
No one awake will tell you that
but Keats.

Drift down. Bye. An altitude
in reverse, a fist
you never learned to make—

Snow is
free fall, you
equal to its gradual, its many
far-off and fade or
secret up this

barely this.

Tool & Shade

A brush of two minds still
comes to one point.

I pick it up in the big-windowed room.
Light for these artists, though
imagine dark here. Imagine how
and because and no matter: you draw
yourself drawing.

Philosophers drink coffee to spin
their webs. Someone else poured that cup
and drove to work late.
A glass pot with its fake silver band could mean
minimum wage, the steam
a sting that she parked wrong, in a hurry
and keeps thinking about the ticket. Heavy,
holding that thing up.

In studio, the sound
of a brush, a conté crayon, a pencil
losing something. Fifteen *whish whishings*
make the quiet
more quiet. It goes on
a long time, a near

nothing, a passing, until the ends —
who cares about ends. I was drawing, wasn't I?
A shape, weird
hurtling up through paper.

There Came a Point in the Brutal Winter

I thought: this is it. We'll never
be different or warmer or crazier than

now in this freeze, not
refreeze either since

nothing will thaw. Like that mythic-real
long continuous of

the Little Ice Age dragging the terrified
through the late Middle Ages

into empty, those who—
The fields in shock, even birds

with so little to eat, song
for no reason, any notion of spring

receding to a pinpoint, how great longing
works a way out. The oldest

trees still speak
its narrow rings if you

take a saw and bear down
weeks, those trunks

a continent to cross.
It must be a kindness, sleep

coming first to the lost
in such cold. House

on a street, town where
day after day the minutes

froze to the clock, then
the clock iced over.

What eternity has to feel like,
hardly anything, no.

Glint

Love is time, sure.

And a window's wiry patch sewn to the screen
a circle cut badly from
spare mesh. The stitching around the tear
makes a circle, makes

a *working* screen because
flies, wasps, even a bat gets into its head to
squeeze pliable out of
late afternoon into a darker house.

A hundred years, this doing it right —

from a practiced hand she
learned it no doubt: *I swear this room
refuge* — worth the clarity, the trouble, a truce for
large and small to come.

If only to lie on a bed and just talk, to look outside

from the original inside. *There,*
says the 20th century before
agony, and early. You weren't
an anything yet.

See how the
inch-by-inch black thread aches, her
fingers cramping up, smallest

glint and how it hides.

Aubade Off-Site, with Mirror and Self

In ur-times, the front parlor
taken over by the dead when the dead died again,
laid out, brief heir to
local tribute, a misnomer, *wake,* given the windows
black-creped, not a leak of light so
the dead would stay dead for the next world,
not escape to the yard. The mirror too,

since one of the lost might be

bedazzled and step through to
stay, far worse than dying,
fixed chronic forever ear-cupping the wall.

Thus the funeral *parlor.* Across town. Off-site
and just so wanna-be-homey, the set for
some overmuch movie, even a *director* looming close
for sorrow and money,
a soaked sponge faux-emoting mist to circle
your private flood.

The house freed up then, broken off from the dead.
For the living. Duh. The *living* room now
though the dead lived there once.

Oh the dead live everywhere.

Which doesn't seem possible
certain mornings. Spring, the birds
out there in endless
blank-maddening repeat some read
as hope. Birds do. Life! Sex! A few

rock-and-roll babies going on,
yes, galore!

As for the ur-universe
in the ur-mirror—is it ever
not shrouded? That face in the way. A mouth.
The big self in there. Those eyes wanting
anywhere but straight

you again? Blocking the view.

I Get to Float Invisible

Someone's sister in Europe writing her
adultery poems late night, half bottle
of wine pretty much required.

And they're good, they really are—

The things one hears in an elevator.
Perfect strangers. I've always loved
the *perfect* part, as if news of the world is

a matter of pitch, and pure.

Maybe the desire of others only
simplifies me, seems generous that way.
It's the distance, an intimacy

so far from here I get to float invisible
all over, over again like I never
lived this life. What could be

lonelier, more full of

mute ringing than what
she's writing. That, and the wine.
Thus we pass the minutes,

ground to five, then six. And the door opens

because someone else pressed
the button first.
All along dark and light

take turns falling to earth.
And the sister
having sipped from a glass

and left behind such small shocks

is no doubt
asleep by now. I forget. Given
the time change.

Island

Moon. Then clouds. And a star
could be planetary, even
a ring around it. Rain is drop
by drop into
morning with its
early, its no need yet.

Out there a boat because
the sound of a boat, a low repeated whistle.
Because one wants to,
one wants.

What's with this
one, doing it all from a distance.

A telescope fixed
on the moon last night. That was
the human part: clouds rushing over it
as if I were
the one at rest.

I Do Not Close the Curtains

Huge windows full of, acting out—

Dark blue run, rim of
pink momentary. There's a fainter blue. What a thing to see
on waking. Or was I waking.

—

J.M.W. Turner. Three brushstrokes. Late in life. The middle
of nothing. He didn't call it painting.
He called it *Boats at Sea*.

I dreamt others laughed: Good God! Why not call it
Men in Fog? And one of them, an aside—wouldn't that be Ruskin?—
no, *Fog in Men*.

—

Birds so *sure of it sure of it sure of it* early.
They have reason. This short life.
And our amusement that they say anything in English.

—

The sky changes—fast. Like you watercolor words, sketch
to keep up with the mind thinning to mist like that thought I had.
Evaporation: water gone missing. The saddest phrase—
a moment ago. Also lost.

—

We think the most obsessive one says *drink your tea*.
But the poignant one, I told my boy its
real story. Oh, you mean like—
singing, he
I-want / a-wife. Ten years old, putting words
in the bird's ache, same
open air two decades later, and counting.

—

Turner, anticipating or in defense:
The only use of the thing is to recall the impression. And the hand
gets that? A brush letting loose,
the paper unconcerned, going blank, so good about it.

—

A weird no-sound. Must be a hawk.
Thus dread, not rest. Either way, we're stitching, stitching
story-starved creatures. Poor sparrow.
Then cacophony comes back.

—

I love that. That Turner—all brilliant famous exactitude—
drifted into disconnect. I like the *idea*.

But I stood at the sea where he stood. It did
keep blurring. Sky barely not water, their difference
by a shade bluish-white between
which is which.
The horizon, pointless after all.

—

Nearly every book in the library on Turner checked out.
Someone else in this town bull's-eye-smitten by his immediate
two hundred years ago. And me—I thought
I was alone with him.

A door, then a street. A carousel in the park
bright with children. Mothers and fathers and babies on blankets.
I imagine them talking: *A little supper but there's*
the whole afternoon still, not for a while. And Turner,
part of this now.

—

Odd obstreperous son of a barber and an hysteric.
Some in their letters,
their journals: a genius that short?

—

No interiors much
I know of. Only his down cliffs
and seascapes, volcanoes, streets, each violent
not-quite aftermath.
Rarely on-site. He worked
in studio. Memory, history, make it up, trove
bigger than paper or canvas or brain or hand or eye
keeps it.

Precision—

go back to
can't. Space then enclosure, enclosure
then space.

Reading in Bed

I'm reading you a poem as you
fall asleep, smallest door inside
to the almost, not quite

cease to be, you and me,

what someone wrote closing
his eyes too, some
woods exactly where
no sound at all in the road
or a leaf, this
dream all along was here

and here you
come to: I *was* listening —

the best way
to honor any poem, waking
up to it, I think.

Photo and Photo and Photo

Muybridge. As if drugged, such staring
the world thought practically pornographic, what
with their skivvies mainly, and too much
workaday flesh.

What he meant, over and over: this
is how we look.
And our take, in our time: you're
sort of like us.

His photographs on repeat, repeat
back in the day, ur-book of stills dreaming of movies
before movies.

Toxic, the 19th century. Muybridge's eye
darkroom eye to deadly and wet, to
mercury, to cyanide. A fraught thing, getting
our plain elegance right. *Like* a man's hammer
coming down in some barnyard, *like* a woman knifing air,
fixed repeatedly to do in a chicken
short of slaughter. She's calm as a needle
over a sampler.

Which is to say, under his black hood Muybridge freezes
each second equal. His catch-and-release all
along these lines. It's addictive
here in the hereafter, to bring back genus and species,
one gesture at a time.

Look at these people.

Oh tightwad camera, saving up for the future. Oh tripod
plus two human legs, trousers, black shoes
under a shroud. And the little done-for pop! and spit!
of the shutter, a spark to small fires.
Thus we lived.

Over and over is key. Over and over
is the saddest thing.

And noble. The elephant folio, a picture book for
a giant. Then I'm the giant. Hover, hover.
Everything he saw glossy-open
on the library floor, the pin-drop stacks, the narrow aisle.

I'm down on all fours, afloat as in: Muybridge
hoped for this, and small
my godlike company.

Six Tuscan Poets

at the Minneapolis Institute of Art

Only three I'll remember.
Because Dante's arm sweeps across the painting's
middle distance of globe, pen,
a sextant on the table.
Because Petrarch's lovesick. Because Boccaccio
is Chaucer on steroids, his misfits
outrunning the plague's dark joke, each stab
of walking stick. *We are all*

pilgrims and strangers. So goes the stone of one
sad sweet German in Rome's
Protestant Cemetery: goodbye Hamburg, your more
bridges than Venice. For that matter, goodbye
my dear dank diseased London, Keats surely called out
over whatever fish in the sea, the ship enroute
to get him better in Rome. Dumb idea. He landed
in that graveyard face-up soon enough.
TB. Only for the best of them. Nineteenth century,
I hate you sometimes.

These Tuscan poets still
talk to each other! Whatever year. 1575 plus now
equals ongoing. In Vasari's great painting
they point to make a point,
take it down and across. Dante's emphatic —
it's Virgil he holds up
with his other beautiful hand. Petrarch fights
a word in. His pal Boccaccio above them, second tier,
looks sideways and off, destined
for the best neighborhood in my house, volume 4,
the 1910 *Britannica* which

loves the Black Death
and dreams his fleeing donkey carts.

Certain days I close my eyes and it's
our seawash, the future looking back at our
little inky spot of watery life-forms
and bad light. Then I think of something else.

Like these three, miraculous and unstuck
in the same room with me.

Track

Trees end at
one curve in the track where
horses famously race

and I took my bike, dodging pines, maples
up to the fence that divides
the washed from the unwashed, those who

pay and who don't but my front tire
doesn't nuzzle each stake and crosswire
like a colt would, can't nibble the grass.

Nothing doing today, too early
in the season plus the gloom of
about-to-rain dims

it all down. The stalls, they
back into these woods too, and one
dejected teenager part-timing it,

about to walk a filly past the bright red
cold-drink machine, no doubt
having rubbed her shiny, speaking out

of his sullen thought-balloon
sweet to this god bred for
perfect and beautiful and quick.

It's not sentimental. They're meant
to the bone to make money.
If one breaks and she falls, it's

unbearable, a great hush
but the inevitable pistol in the dark
of a car will be mentioned.

I've heard our kind, one
of the old
looking up blithely —*save one for me!*—

to news of anyone's massive
heart attack. And doesn't the track
sometimes starry-end a night race

with such fireworks? Which to horses
must seem terror point-blank and
blank so high, a million

multiples of the starting gun that
shocked into another life
in the first place.

If Only

How certain mice in winter's tall grass
wildly off and on
ultraviolet because the red-shouldered hawk sees
delicious in that dim, one very hungry
X-ray machine on the prowl,
the hawk, sort of a genius. Poor mouse never
to imagine its own deadly brilliance or
a chance to change places.

But there's Kafka
kicking himself daily for not
being Dickens. Meanwhile a tiger, higher than mouse
on the fellow-mammal food chain—
he waits two days to do in
a hunter who wounds him into hiding,
into licking himself nonstop.
That's news? That's radio news, 6 a.m., a little
oatmeal on the side.

I conclude: memory is a curse. Even the tiger
is prey to misery's
to-do list, how Kafka wanted a shrewd, generous Dickens
so badly in his bloodstream via some
noisy intricate plot aimed at pompous evil undone.
A giant insect
swallowed him instead. In bed. As for Dickens,
eyes open all night—Miss Havisham's sweet-tedious
ghosting that moldy wedding cake again—he
must have ached for Dante, would have
followed his one lit candle straight to hell to clever those
suicides into trees
quick and stilled as a world without end chilled

hot to the bone. Is it always like this?
Sad, then it isn't at all,

to let the hawk go. And the mouse.

Yeah, but that
thread in the first place flashing old
weeds, dark bitten by an early moon, blood wish,
each blade and each leaf—

Future Lives of the Past

You practice that crazy new thing—Am I cat
or dog?—mammal dream one genus-jumping afternoon
I got to be calico, a three-color whirl
madly off to find better digs, renamed in a fit of
weak brilliance Fabio the Lesser,
loved to death in some hovel, second century, last
purr to be proud of, one final faint meow.
But I was the kid who thought dogs
were boys, cats were girls.

Every possible
strains in us: race, religion, countries of origin
have their own fistfights, gun battles, near
nuclear in the crosshairs. The real
huge of it, lost grandmothers whatever shade of
fearless, clueless, the bullying, the sweet.
To love glazed again, pre-zombie
as childhood. Sleep well, all the grand rest of them.

A word that survives triumphant: *singlet,*
like *islet* in the sea's roar. Full blast who-they-are,
a whole splendid species unto each
puzzling self to loom among those who walk
with Memory, the first Muse.

An extension cord isn't a snake. Memory,
that mother of Muses also says: I've watched
people all my life pick up
and put down that snake. Then plug it into a wall.

The human predicament, about a million pounds
not counting the arms

holding us upright three thousand years plus,
plus I started early, color and gender unknown,
a bent Neanderthal
given my stricken awe before
the scary, the blood ax, thunder
as code misery, code danger to come.

Future lives of the past, past lives of the future
rough beast it again. Gobsmacked
congrats that we all made it through to this moment.

Is it me, or am I
a many, I ask the square peg and round hole in my head

because those two really
should talk one of these days, day it comes down to
amazement and relief.

A Translation of Frogs

A translation on the frogs: too much
to eat or drink but really
wannabe and will you yes yes
all night, this every hour booming
blaring an urgent reckon, to bring on what
keeps the old old and separate from the young,
the long view for some vs. sweet
crazy straight-up agony.

To hear the loudest among them in spring
is to imagine
jowls on that creature not even legal, his
castaway lovesick bellow across water.
Not jowls, of course.

In this I honor the pond so
backdrop and sheen
wholly discreet under moonlight.

What Held the Cathedral Aloft

Muffled to telepathy, blood never
talks outright to heart.
Still the dumbest things

pass my lips because I just
want to hear you
say again. Not to *get* it.

It's the *getting,* rush-tunnel of
cooler water in water
when we were

swimming that time. But fish,
their all color
slow motion, beginning

and end ever
no sound who they are
in lit blue. Like —

no disrespect to
the cornerstone — the flying buttress
holds the cathedral aloft.

I won't say lift. Nothing
leaves the ground for good.
Love, I won't

say the heart
a ridiculous muscle either —
lopsided, pretty boring,

repeating itself senseless all
every long reach,
lower limb to brain to

what becomes of us, inner
ear and pulse hushed
blood at a slant.

Whole Conversations as a Creature Almost Credible

Whole conversations I've had as
a creature almost credible, not even looking at a face.

Sometimes I hear, I even listen.
I tilt my head just so to
picture the dance recital minutely,
the mother-in-law's birthday party, thorns
on roses, leaves turning
their yellow and sad red-glorious.

I'm sorry, I say, I'm sorry, as if my
to the side and down matters for a second.

It's not like it was a surprise, she's saying back.

And it isn't like a heartbeat really does
fit the scanner, like any room can be unlocked.

A hallway, a regular workday. The two of us
bending toward, our distance's worth
of low voice, half
an arm's length, the hesitation
of a fragment: *and when he?* and *so good you could...*

You could. And maybe in a hundred years I could.

Had she taken off her glasses? Was she blinking too much,
this close to blurring —

The many things to unlearn. Like, come off it.
Never *we* in that expanse.

Walking Backwards

to go forward, to take it in again, everything you left.
And the woods for this. A rehearsal, of sorts,
the trail crosshatched sticks and roots, the danger minutely
huge. So I trip. I could fall.

I did it for real once or twice—walked backwards,
a weirdo among trees.
My brain clicked its socket. Pins sharpened in my head.

For real, I saw ancient black oaks go forlornly
sudden, that angle. Then *Who says? You?*
Good riddance to me, mere
passerby in the leaf mold, holding on with my
looking, my what-have-you.

Some gestures *mean,* they're symbol,
god forbid, allegory, i.e.—bigger than they are
or ever will be. The past. You turn and twist to figure
any of it. By now the stillness
has already eaten you or banished you or
something. You, the nerve, the gall,
your know-it-all flashlight aimed in reverse as if
any place you'd leave
goes dark, howbeit and really. Someone pipes up—
really?

Two words for this: shelf life. Or four: little pantry, old house.
Where I wait out storms with the dead
who still have names. Swear to god, I loved it there.

The Art of Poetry

isn't sleep. Isn't the clock's steady
one and one and one though seconds eventually make
an hour. And morning passes
into a thing it might not recognize by afternoon.

Or you practice the ordinary art
of shrinking strangers back to children, who they
could have been: bangs straight across,
boys and girls the same.
I blink kids into grown-ups too, who they
might be, the exaggerated gestures we do,
the weight on each word
a warning, kindly
or just so full of ourselves
we can't help it. But this oddest

not old or young, male, female,
this century or that—it simply
visits. This who, this
what. This art
of suspension. Wait.

If you've ever acted, you understand what it is,
standing in the wings, the dark
murmur out there. Every dream
for days you nightmare that. Saying or not saying.
Then wake to lights, the other
pretenders on stage bowing, happy enough.
Except it's not

like that, this wish
being small: to make emptiness

an occasion, the art of calling it down.
To wonder for the first time *as I write it*. And elegant
is good. And story. And edgy
half-uttered in fragments is good. Always that
sense of the dead overhearing. Or simply: voice I never,
not once in the world, give me a sign.
I'll pick up the thread. Dally with it, sit in its coma,
wait for its news in the little room
off the nurses' station. Don't be

maudlin, says the garden, don't
be pretty pretty pretty, and don't think whimsy
unto irony disguises.
Because it is
a garden. You walk and walk and twilight now,
its darker half
half-floats a yellow still visible in high spiky things.

There's a dovecote where nothing nests. There's an expanse
orderly as blueprint but flowers get wily, only
make believe they agree the best place
to stand or lean. It's not the sun.
I can't decide anything. Can't decide.

Begging bowl, ask
until asking is a stain. Every garden's a mess.
Am I poised at an angle? Am I listening?
A stillness so
different than winter's, lush and forgetful though

all the lost summers lie in it. Old photographs,
children a century ago who
never thought to leave still busy
fading into sepia, making houses in the yard out of
porch chairs tipped over,
and sheets. Their worn shirts, their hair every

which way. Someone loved them.
She raised a camera.

But I don't,
don't mean that. It's the art of the makeshift
almost house. Or how the children
don't see her, so aren't
dear yet.

Aubade Under

notes from the fog which
by definition leaves no notes. No earthly possession
of mind allowed. Blurred illegal, not
accountable, murder

weapon-o'-vapor, a lot of split-second indecision.

Violet or pink, some kind of
sunrise through trees — definitely

a brain-blanking that you know but just can't see it.

The fog wrote: *Yet another thing that doesn't matter!*
This whole ball of wax is
full of them. I can't even show you the car.

Fog means the red one it hates, toxic-dazzled as
ambition is, going too fast, people telling you

for sure, for sure anything. *Forget it! I don't give a flying*

you know what! writes the fog, its penmanship
forlorn as cursive left to
don't even bother now. Which is only to say
you can take that damn anything — hear the fog? — *and put it...*

Name the spot! I wise-guyed, on the spot.

(Sophomoric, yeah. Forgive me. I'm eking out a moment
between former lives: human sleep and up all night.)

That's the fog for you, the fog sang as
eye of a needle to the end of the world. Chanted forever,
for ten minutes. *I'm such*

a generous start from scratch, come back never ever sort of
first-rate phenomenon! I hold! I hover! I burn off by 8!

Yes, phenomenon, a hermit, blind blue streak, a monk —

The Sound and Silence of the World Now

One of them, a black-marketeer hoarding chocolate
and mayonnaise, acquired
god knows, hero of the neighborhood party, some place
hard to pronounce, on radio
all that cheering and static across mountains and cities
and wires and rivers unto ocean and airspace and star-studded orbits—
alone in my kitchen is the sound

and silence of the world now. How not to love
his generous graft? How not to be the small child or that
ancient one endless and again her story about the cat,
or the clear-eyed, bad-tempered
old guy of lament and rue and I-told-you-so
enraptured by the sudden what a score

middle of winter, deep snow in this village I never heard of but
could lie twisted in my gene pool, that wily
spool of fortune. At least thirty people! A single lit house
on a street of houses, nine bicycles this cold, three motorbikes, one
shiny car, one rusting out near the ditch. How not to
invent more, to see him pull that sweet-heavy dark from his pack
and what will make the thick black bread
soaked through, lovely mess. He holds it high as fable—oh chocolate,

the very best, and mayonnaise too. And who
can't see plainly more cheers, the welcome everyone of it,
the well come, the have some, you go first, little one—

Here. Where outside the yard has doubled in crows if you count
their shadows in the drifts but I will not
and I do not for a while.

Acknowledgments

For David Dunlap, "The Young Husband," "Song in Winter," "Singular," and "What Held the Cathedral Aloft"; for Joan, Will, and Forrest Dunlap, "Little Handheld, Little Movie in a Phone."

"Photo and Photo and Photo" is for Michael Boruch, with thanks for his thoughts on the history of photography.

"Aubade Under" is for Rosanna Bruno and Anne-E Wood, "The Ice Floe" for Susan Neville, and for Jill Quirk, the poem "Divide."

"Before and Every After" is in memory of James A. Judkins.

"Private Garden, Open to the Public" is for Jane Hamilton, and its second italicized bit paraphrases Nora Ephron. The piece refers to (and first quotes from) a memorial sculpture at Yaddo, a place—I say this with much appreciation—where several poems in this collection were written. Equal gratitude to the Anderson Center, Red Wing, Minnesota, for its shelter and solace as I wrote.

Thanks to David Deschamps for musical facts that helped me with "Notation Gregorian," to Rodney Jones for the news about Kafka's secret brought into "If Only," and to Connie Voisine, who introduced me to the desert referenced in the first and last of the Dickinson poems here, specifically Las Cruces, New Mexico, and the oldest house in that area built by the Maes family in the 1840s (now the Double Eagle restaurant).

"Triptych in Grief and Life-Glad" touches on information in Nadezhda Mandelstam's *Hope Against Hope: A Memoir,* brought out of the Russian by Max Hayward (New York: Atheneum, 1970). "Endlessly *zhizneradostny,*" Mandelstam's wife calls her husband. As Clarence Brown explains in the introduction, "the word is usually rendered as 'cheerful' or 'joyous,'" its two parts literally meaning "life-glad."

I also want to acknowledge an audio set of brilliant lectures, Teofilo F. Ruiz's *Medieval Europe: Crisis and Renewal* (Virginia: The Teaching Company, 1996), which put me so deep in dream I missed three important turns on a long drive east. Later that dream influenced "Progress," "Notation Gregorian," "When I Think about the First Pope to Quit," and "There Came a Point in the Brutal Winter."

Behind the poem "a" is a visit to the Wolverine Press at the University of Michigan, Ann Arbor, where I learned from its director, Fritz Swanson, of the chronic overuse of the letter *a* in the old letterpress machines. Nicola Mason of *The Cincinnati Review,* and later Daniel Hubbs of the Saratoga Springs Public Library, helped me with facts concerning "I Do Not Close the Curtains."

About the epigraph for this book, a phrase from a late version of John Berryman's *Dream Songs,* the word "they" to be altered to "then" in the published collection: I thank Rachel Reynolds, a poet in my graduate workshop at Purdue, fall 2014, who introduced us to those pages generously shared with her by the University of Minnesota Library's Manuscript Division.

Many thanks to the editors of the following publications who first took a chance on these poems, at times in an earlier form: The Academy of American Poets' *Poem-a-Day, The American Poetry Review, Arts & Letters, The Cincinnati Review, Crazyhorse, Denver Quarterly, Edinburgh Review, Field, The Georgia Review, Great River Review, The Hampden-Sydney Poetry Review, The Kenyon Review, The Massachusetts Review, Michigan Quarterly Review, The Nation, New England Review, The New Yorker, The New York Review of Books, Ploughshares, Plume, Poetry, Poetry London, TriQuarterly,* and *Volt.* "The Art of Poetry," appearing initially in *Pilot Light,* received a Pushcart Prize in 2013; "Mudfest" received a Pushcart in 2016, appearing first in *APR.* "I Get to Float Invisible," which appeared first in *The Georgia Review,* was chosen for *The Best American Poetry 2016.* "Six Tuscan Poets" appeared in *The Plume Poetry Anthology, Volume 4* (MadHat Press, 2016).

Much gratitude to the Fulbright Foundation, to Surgeons' Hall, Edinburgh, Scotland, to the University of Edinburgh, and to Purdue University for crucial aid and abetting. And to Margaret Rowe, Eleanor Wilner, and Wendy Flory for their response to work in this collection.

And of course, of course, loving thanks to David Dunlap and Will Dunlap, ongoing and from the start.

About the Author

Marianne Boruch's eight previous poetry collections include *Cadaver, Speak* (2014) and *The Book of Hours* (2011), a Kingsley-Tufts Poetry Award winner, both from Copper Canyon Press. She's also published a memoir, *The Glimpse Traveler* (Indiana, 2011), about hitchhiking in the early 1970s, and two essay collections on poetry, *In the Blue Pharmacy* (Trinity, 2005) and *Poetry's Old Air* (Michigan, 1995). A third volume, *The Little Death of Self: Nine Essays toward Poetry* is forthcoming from Michigan. Her work has appeared in *The American Poetry Review, Field, London Review of Books, Narrative, The Nation, The New York Review of Books, The New Yorker, Ploughshares, Poetry,* and elsewhere. Three of her poems have been chosen for *Best American Poetry;* four have received Pushcart Prizes.

Twice a National Endowment for the Arts Fellow, Boruch also has been awarded a Guggenheim Fellowship and artist residencies at the Rockefeller Foundation's Bellagio Center, Yaddo, the MacDowell Colony, the Anderson Center (Red Wing, Minnesota), at Denali in Alaska, and Isle Royale, our most isolated national park. In 2015, she was given the Indiana Writers Award (national division) by the Glick Foundation. A 2012 Fulbright/Visiting Professor in Scotland at the University of Edinburgh, she was the founding director of Purdue University's MFA program in the English department where she still teaches and, since 1988, has been semiregularly on faculty at the low-residency Program for Writers at Warren Wilson College. She and her husband, David Dunlap, live in West Lafayette, Indiana, where they raised their son.

Poetry is vital to language and living. Since 1972, Copper Canyon Press has published extraordinary poetry from around the world to engage the imaginations and intellects of readers, writers, booksellers, librarians, teachers, students, and donors.

WE ARE GRATEFUL FOR THE MAJOR SUPPORT PROVIDED BY:

THE PAUL G. ALLEN
FAMILY FOUNDATION

Anonymous

Donna and Matt Bellew

John Branch

Diana Broze

Janet and Les Cox

Beroz Ferrell & The Point, LLC

Alan Gartenhaus and Rhoady Lee

Mimi Gardner Gates

Linda Gerrard and Walter Parsons

Gull Industries, Inc.
on behalf of William and Ruth True

Mark Hamilton and Suzie Rapp

Carolyn and Robert Hedin

Steven Myron Holl

Lakeside Industries, Inc.
on behalf of Jeanne Marie Lee

TO LEARN MORE ABOUT UNDERWRITING
COPPER CANYON PRESS TITLES,
PLEASE CALL 360-385-4925 EXT. 103

WE ARE GRATEFUL FOR THE MAJOR SUPPORT PROVIDED BY:

Maureen Lee and Mark Busto

Brice Marden

Ellie Mathews and Carl Youngmann as The North Press

H. Stewart Parker

Penny and Jerry Peabody

John Phillips and Anne O'Donnell

Joseph C. Roberts

Cynthia Lovelace Sears and Frank Buxton

The Seattle Foundation

Kim and Jeff Seely

David and Catherine Eaton Skinner

Dan Waggoner

C.D. Wright and Forrest Gander

Charles and Barbara Wright

The dedicated interns and faithful volunteers of Copper Canyon Press

The Chinese character for poetry is made up of two parts: "word"
and "temple." It also serves as pressmark for Copper Canyon Press.

This book is set in Bembo Book MT Pro, a digital recasting of
Bembo, a Venetian typeface from the 1500s. Book design by
VJB/Scribe. Printed on archival-quality paper.